my first fruits
in modern greek

translated by Lydia Kopanou

polyglot kids

μήλο

MEE-loh

apple

αχλάδι

akh-LAH-thee

pear

σταφύλι

stah-FEE-lee

grape

σύκο

SEE-koh

fig

μούρο

MOO-roh

mulberry

δαμάσκηνο

thah-MAH-skee-noh

plum

κεράσι

keh-RAH-see

cherry

ροδάκινο

roh-THAH-kee-noh

peach

ρόδι

ROH-thee

pomegranate

πεπόνι

peh-POH-nee

melon

© 2025 by Polyglot Kids Books / World Poetry Books
Photography © 2025 by Sebastian Fröhlich

Series editors: Peter Constantine & Hannes Schumacher
Translated into Modern Greek by Lydia Kopanou
Photography: Sebastian Fröhlich
Design: Hannes Schumacher & Sebastian Fröhlich
ISBN: 978-1-967821-10-5

Polyglot Kids Books is an imprint of World Poetry Books, Inc. New York.

www.ingramcontent.com/pod-product-compliance
Lightning Source LLC
Chambersburg PA
CBHW061355010526
44107CB00012B/944

Olivia's New Friend

Monique Jenkins   PhD, MA, APRN, FNP-BC, FNYAM

Copyright© 2025.
MONIQUE JENKINS PhD, MA, APRN, FNP-BC, FNYAM
All Rights Reserved.

Illustrated by Valeria Chairez Ramos

ISBN: 978-1-961600-51-5
Library of Congress Control Number: 2025907132

FIG FACTOR MEDIA

Dedication

To My Family - your unwavering love, patience and belief in me have been a constant source of strength. Thank you for encouraging my dreams, understanding the long hours and celebrating every victory along the way. Your support has carried me through more than words can express.

To My Colleagues - it is an honor to work alongside such dedicated and compassionate professionals. Your tireless commitment to excellence and your ability to bring comfort, skill and humanity into the most challenging moments never ceases to amaze and inspire me. I am grateful for the collaboration and shared purpose we hold in caring for our vulnerable population of patients.

Most of all, to the pediatric surgical patients and their families - your resilience, courage and grace in the face of uncertainty are the true heartbeat of this book. In your most vulnerable moments, you show what true bravery looks like. Thank you for allowing me into your lives, for trusting me with your care and for reminding me every day why this work matters. Your stories will always stay with me and this book is a tribute to the unwavering hope you so beautifully embody.

Hi, My name is Olivia!

I love playing with my toys, eating yummy food, and having adventures.

But today, I'm going to tell you about a special new friend who helps me every day!

ONE DAY, I didn't feel well. My tummy hurt a lot, and I didn't feel like playing.

Mommy and Daddy took me to the doctor to find out what was wrong.

Graaak!

The doctor said

I had a sick belly and needed something called a stoma to help my tummy feel better. A stoma is like a little magic button that helps me go poop without any pain. He said I would need it only for a little while. Just until the intestines in my belly healed and felt better.

at the hospital, I woke up with my new friend. It's a small bag that sticks to my tummy, and it's very important. I named my bag "Buddy" because it helps me every day.

Buddy and I

do everything together. We play, eat, and even sleep together. Buddy collects my poop, so I don't have to worry about it. It's kind of like having a secret helper!

Every day,
Mom helps me change Buddy to keep it clean. It's a little sticky, but it doesn't hurt. We have a routine: we clean my tummy, put on a new bag, and then we're ready for more fun.
I'm going to show you how to take care of Buddy.

First, we need to get our supplies ready. We need a new bag, some cleaning wipes, scissors and skin protector. Only mommy can use the scissors. I'm not allowed. Let's get started!

STEP 1:

Gently take off the old bag. Be careful and take your time. It might feel a little sticky, but that's okay! We use a special wipe to make it come off easier.

STEP 2:

Clean around the stoma. Use soft wipes to clean the skin. Make sure it's nice and clean so Buddy can stick properly.

STEP 3:

Put on the skin protector. This helps keep the skin healthy and makes sure Buddy sticks well. It's like giving your tummy a hug!

STEP 4:

Cut a hole the size of the "magic button" stoma.

STEP 5:

Place the new bag. Carefully stick the new bag over the stoma. Make sure it's snug and secure so it doesn't leak.

new bag

All done! Now Buddy is ready for more adventures. Changing the bag is easy when you know the steps!

with Buddy

taken care of, I can run, jump, and play without any worries. It's important to keep Buddy clean and comfy so we can have fun together.

Remember, you're never alone. Your family and friends are always there to help you take care of your ostomy. And with a little practice, you and your family will be pros in no time!

Having an ostomy doesn't stop me from doing anything I love. I can run, jump, and play just like before. Buddy makes sure my tummy stays happy and healthy.

So, that's the story of me and my new friend Buddy. If you ever need an ostomy or know somebody who has an ostomy, just remember, it's there to help you feel better and keep having amazing adventures!

And remember what I said before, you're never alone! Your family, friends, and Buddy will always be there to help you. Stay happy and keep smiling!

An Ostomy Word Search

```
W I P E S T T S T O M A A A A
I R R R R R R O S R R T R T
O S T O M Y T Y L T G G A G A
D D D L D D D I O D D P D P
S C I S S O R S V M S S E S E
G G G G G S G G I Y G G G G G
O O S T O M Y B A G H H H H H
I V W O E A D H E S I V E V E
S K I N P R O T E C T O R O R
B U D D Y Y C C C O I O O O O
A D H E S I V E R E M O V E R
```

- Scissors
- Ostomy
- Stoma
- Skin Protector
- Wipes
- Ostomy Bag
- Buddy
- Olivia
- Tape
- Adhesive Remover

Notes for Feelings

About the Author

Monique Jenkins, PhD, MA, FNP-BC, FNYAM, is a nurse practitioner, educator, and author with a deep passion for caring for children and empowering families. With almost two decades of experience in pediatric surgical nursing, she has dedicated her career to helping young patients feel safe, supported, and understood during their medical journeys. She believes that stories have the power to educate, comfort, and inspire, which is why she is devoted to writing books that encourage children to embrace their uniqueness, overcome challenges, and dream big.

As a healthcare leader, Dr. Jenkins has contributed to national guidelines, mentored aspiring nurses & nurse practitioners, and served as President of the only national nursing association focused on those who care for pediatric surgical patients and their families. She has written numerous articles in nursing journals, but her greatest joy comes from sharing stories that help children and families navigate the world with confidence and resilience. Through her books, Dr. Jenkins hopes to spark curiosity, promote kindness, and give children a sense of belonging. She understands the importance of representation in literature and strives to create characters and stories that reflect the diversity of the world around us.

When she's not writing or caring for patients, Dr. Jenkins enjoys mentoring youth & nurses, engaging in community service, and spending time with her family in Brooklyn, New York. She loves exploring new places, practicing yoga and finding inspiration in everyday moments.

Her mission is simple: to make every child feel seen, heard, and valued—one story at a time.

www.ingramcontent.com/pod-product-compliance
Lightning Source LLC
Chambersburg PA
CBHW061356010526
44107CB00012B/945